MUSLIMS
IN BRITAIN

Fiona Macdonald

Consultant: Ajaz Ahmed

Photography by Chris Fairclough

W

FRANKLIN WATTS
LONDON•SYDNEY

First published in 2005 by
Franklin Watts
96 Leonard Street
London
EC2A 4XD

Franklin Watts Australia
Level 17/207 Kent Street
Sydney NSW 2000

A CIP catalogue record for this book
is available from the British Library
Dewey number 305.6'97'041

Planning and production by Discovery Books Limited
Editor: Kate Taylor
Designer: Rob Norridge

The author, packager and publisher would like to thank the
following people for their participation in this book: The Qureshi
family, Bobbersmill Community Centre, Nottingham Islamia
School, Mr Iqbal, Umani, Royals, Moguls.

Photo acknowledgements: P.6, Bettmann/Corbis; P.7, Hulton-
Deutsch Collection/Corbis; P.19 (bottom), Picimpact/Corbis;
P.26, Ferran Paredes/Reuters/Corbis; P.27, AFP/Getty Images;
P.29, Corbis; All others supplied by Chris Fairclough

ISBN: 0 7496 5887 8

Printed in Dubai

Contents

British and Muslim

Around 2 million Muslim men, women and children live in Britain today. All are followers of Islam, the world's second largest religion. But they are only a small minority within Britain, numbering just 4 per cent of the population.

Backgrounds

Like other Britons, Muslim people have different ethnic heritages: Asian, African and European. They respect different traditions, passed on by their ancestors. They speak many different languages, as well as English. Many also study Arabic – the language of the Holy Qur'an.

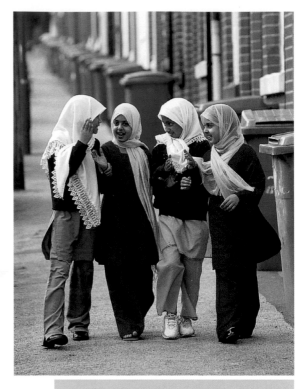

British Muslims have helped to turn the country into the vibrant, multicultural society it is today.

A growing religion

Most British Muslims come from Muslim families, and were born into their faith. But thousands of men and women in Britain, from other faith backgrounds or with no previous religion, have become converts to Islam. It is the fastest-growing religion in Britain – and the world.

The crescent moon is the symbol of Islam. It can be seen on mosques throughout the world.

> **One can be a British Muslim and still maintain a strong affinity [love for] your city or town.... We should continue our efforts to build a peaceful, strong and influential British Muslim community.**
>
> *University student Nayala Rehmat.*

Britain's workforce

Muslims play an active part in all areas of British life. Some are highly educated, with well-paid, professional careers. Many own shops or run factories, or work in caring professions such as teaching and medicine. Some are entertainers, journalists, engineers or experts in information technology.

There are Muslim MPs, Muslim members of the House of Lords, Muslim MEPs and Muslim mayors, together with hundreds of Muslim local councillors, political campaigners, welfare workers and community volunteers.

Price £1.50

The
INVITATION
Muslim Family Magazine

Page 20: The Macshane Shame:
After Denis Macshane made shameful remarks telling British Muslims to choose their way instead of terrorism, an Invitation reader writes about the shameful response from his local mosques

Page 22: Foreign Policy
Aid has always been an instrument of foreign policy and driven by commerce, so aid sometimes goes to the manufacturers direct!! George Monbiot explains

Page 24: A Story from Iraq
Like other dictatorships and regimes, the US military has now followed suit in Iraq by attempting to select what its personnel should and should not read.

There are several British newspapers and magazines specially published for the Muslim community.

Arriving and settling

There have been contacts between Britain and Muslim lands for over one thousand years. In the Middle Ages, British scholars studied the works of Muslim writers, and Britons traded with Muslim merchants. The first English translation of the Muslim holy book, the Qur'an, was printed in 1649.

Making Britain a permanent home

Muslim men and women have been arriving to live in Britain for centuries. Many were seamen who settled in British ports. The first-known British mosque (Muslim place of worship) was established in Cardiff, Wales, around 1860.

The first major migration of Muslims to Britain came in the 1920s, when Arabs from the Persian Gulf region came to settle here. They were followed after World War II (1939–45) by Muslim men from the Indian subcontinent – now India, Pakistan and Bangladesh. These Muslims came to fill job vacancies, as Britain tried to rebuild its post-war economy. Originally, many intended to return home after a while. But later most sent for their families to join them, and settled here permanently.

DID YOU KNOW?

Over 600 English words are of Arabic origin, including admiral, elephant, lemon, magazine and traffic.

With no mosques nearby, many of the first Muslims to settle in Britain had to worship outside. This meeting took place in April 1922.

6

As the Muslim community in Britain and Europe grew larger, leaders set up organisations such as the Islamic Council of Europe. These met to discuss problems and plan policies.

Escaping crisis

In the 1970s and 1980s, Muslim families expelled from Kenya and Uganda came to Britain to escape persecution. Political dissidents, professionals, business people and students came from Nigeria, Cyprus, Turkey and Muslim lands in the Middle East as well. In the 1990s, Muslims fled to Britain from Somalia, Bosnia, Kosovo, Afghanistan and Iraq, to escape hunger and war. Today, small numbers of Muslims still arrive to settle in Britain, but more than half of all British Muslims (around 55 per cent) were born here.

There were no Indian families at that time – it was men only until the 1950s and 1960s. I had to stay with other men at a lodging house in the city. The first job I did...was loading a goods train for British Railways. Everybody was friendly.

Mohamad Sahrif, from Lahore, describes his life in Birmingham during World War II.

The faith of Islam

The word 'Islam' means 'Peace' or 'submission' to God. Followers of Islam are called Muslims (people who obey God's will). They believe that there is only one true God, Allah.

Muslim men kneel to say prayers at a British mosque.

The Prophet Muhammad

Muslims honour the Prophet Muhammad, a religious leader who lived in Arabia from around 570–632 CE. They believe he was the last of the holy prophets (messengers sent by Allah to show humans how to live) and that there will be no more prophets after him. To show their love for the Prophet Muhammad, many British Muslim families name their sons after him.

SUNNI AND SHIA

Over the centuries, the worldwide Muslim community has divided. There are Sunni and Shia Muslims. Today, the differences between the two are more to do with politics than religion.

Qur'an

Muslims also revere the Qur'an, an Arabic text revealed to the Prophet Muhammad by Allah, through the angel Gabriel. The Qur'an is in Arabic, the language spoken by the prophet Muhammad, and was written down after he died. Muslims believe the Qur'an is the Word of Allah, and that it teaches them how to live good lives.

Devout study

Today in Britain, Muslims study the Qur'an, and recite verses from it as an act of devotion. Muslim children go to Qur'an schools, held after ordinary lessons or at weekends. They learn to read the Qur'an in Arabic and memorise passages from it.

Older members of the Muslim community believe it is an important religious duty to teach young Muslims to read and memorise the Qur'an.

Living as a Muslim

Muslims believe that all their actions should be guided by their faith. For six days each week, Muslims pray at home, at work or at school. On Fridays especially, men and boys go to mosques to say communal prayers and to listen to an imam (a religious teacher).

There are nearly 600 registered mosques in Britain, and many unregistered rooms where Muslims meet to pray. Traditionally, women and girls do not go to mosques, but in some British Muslim communities they join in Friday worship, where they sit and pray in a private section apart from the men.

A muezzin broadcasts the call to prayer from the mosque.

Five Pillars of Islam

Traditionally, Muslims put their faith into practice in five different ways – these are called the 'Five Pillars of Islam'. The first pillar is Shahadah (declaration of belief) – 'There is no god but Allah, and Muhammad is His Prophet.'

This prayer-clock lets Muslims know the right time to say their daily prayers.

The second pillar is Salah, prayers said five times a day, before dawn, at mid-day, mid-afternoon and sunset, and at night before midnight. In Britain, prayer times vary from summer to winter, depending on the length of daylight. British Muslims consult special calendars, or Muslim websites, to check prayer times. If they have mobile phones, they may use text-message reminder services.

PRAYER

Before praying, Muslims wash their face, hands and feet. This is called 'wudu'. To say prayers, Muslims around the world turn their faces to the Ka'bah, which is in the holy city of Makkah, in Saudi Arabia. They bow and kneel during prayer, to show their obedience to Allah.

Zakah

The third pillar of Islam is Zakah – giving money to charity. All Muslims who have more than enough to meet their own basic needs must give 2.5 per cent of their wealth to the poor. In Britain, there are over 100 Muslim charities.

Sawm

Sawm (fasting during daylight hours in the holy month of Ramadan) is the fourth pillar of Islam. By going without food, drink or other pleasures, Muslims learn self-discipline. They also think about people who are hungry or suffering, and how to help them. They thank Allah for the gift of food. People who are old or ill, mothers with babies, and young children are all excused from fasting.

Muslim children learn Arabic so they can fully understand their faith.

Hajj

The fifth pillar of Islam is Hajj (pilgrimage). All Muslims hope to make a journey to the holy city of Makkah, where the Prophet Muhammad first preached the faith of Islam. Muslim travel agents organise special trips to take British Muslims there.

British Muslims

Because British Muslims come from so many different backgrounds, there is no one style of dress, traditional music or typical meal.

Clothes

Muslim men and women are commanded by the Qur'an to dress modestly in public. Women traditionally wear a hijab, or headscarf, to cover their heads. Men keep themselves covered from the waist to the knee and women are required to wear loose clothing which covers them modestly, only revealing their hands and face.

Women from Pakistan often wear salwar kameez (long tunics with baggy trousers), but women from Bangladesh traditionally wear saris. Women from the Middle East and Africa usually wear various loose, baggy garments.

A Muslim worker handmakes dresses and other garments out of material selected by his customers. This store in Nottingham is popular with non-Muslims too.

Radio stations in cities with Muslim communities broadcast music, news and views from Muslim lands worldwide.

Music

British Muslim teenagers enjoy listening to music in Urdu as well as popular British songs. Music from artists in Pakistan, such as Najum Sheraz, Junaid Jamshed, Nusrat Fateh and Ali Khan are all popular. World Music that blends traditional and Western styles is also enjoyed in Britain. Community groups organise programmes and hold classes for children to learn the Nasheed and Naats (singing and chanting religious songs).

A Muslim family meets to share a meal at the end of a busy day.

Food

Food and fasting play an important part in Muslim life. There is a strong tradition of hospitality among Muslim families; sharing food with guests, or needy people, is a religious duty. Fasting is also one of the essential practices of Islam (see page 11).

Most Muslims do not drink alcohol or eat pork. Muslims only eat halal (permitted) meat, which is killed according to Muslim ritual, by cutting the main throat vein. There are many shops in Britain selling halal meat. Muslims eat 20 per cent of all lamb sold in Britain and a similar proportion of traditional foods such as dates and spices. A lot of Indian restaurants are run by Muslims and dishes such as tandoori chicken and lamb kebab have become popular throughout Britain.

Sports

Sport is a passion for many Muslim men – and some women, too. Cricket, football, badminton, basketball and hockey all attract many spectators. Muslims also play in local and national teams. Recently, two Muslim boxers, Javaid Khalique and teenage star Amir Khan, have made headlines.

A Muslim home

There are around 350,000 Muslim households in Britain. Like other British families, British Muslims do not all live in the same way. But many share the traditional belief that a home should be a centre of Islamic values. It is also the place where Muslims can follow traditional faith-based customs – such as sharing halal food – in peace, comfort and security.

Large families

On average, Muslim households are the largest in Britain – many parents have four children or more. One in two Muslims in Britain today is under 24 years old. In a recent survey, around half of all young Muslims said they would also like large families when they grew up and married.

Different generations

Many Muslim households contain three generations – grandparents, parents and children. Traditionally, adult sons live in their parents' home, and bring their wives to live there when they marry. But this pattern is changing, especially among wealthy Muslims with professional careers, who choose to buy their own house when they marry.

A Muslim family smile for the camera outside their home.

Sense of community

In British towns and cities, many Muslim
families live close together in the same
districts. Extended families may live
in neighbouring houses.

Muslim migrants in Britain
often live near people who
belong to the same faith,
follow similar traditions and
understand their language. They go to
Muslim-owned shops selling imported
foods, clothes, books and newspapers
and rely on other Muslim families
for help, advice and friendship
when they feel isolated in an
unfamiliar land.

I arrived here seven years ago from Mirpur, in Pakistan. Although it
is a long way away, Britain feels like home to me now. I am
surrounded by people from the same city as me back in Pakistan who
have the same values and speak the same language. I also get to go
back every couple of years and visit the rest of my family.

Ajaz Ahmed, Nottingham.

Children
and growing up

The first word a Muslim baby hears is 'Allah' (God). They are welcomed into the world with the call to prayer that begins 'Allah is most great'. A ceremony called 'Aquiqah' is held a few days after the birth, when an animal is sacrificed. One third of the meat is given to the poor, one third to relatives and the rest to the family.

Many Muslim girls choose to wear a headscarf (called hijab, or 'covering') with their school uniform.

When a child is ready to begin learning, aged around three or four, some parents hold a 'Bismillah' ceremony, when they teach their child to recite the first words of the Qur'an from memory.

School

Most British Muslim children attend state schools. They learn alongside pupils from all faiths. There are four state-run Muslim schools in Britain, where Muslim education is provided free. Pupils say prayers together, study Arabic and the Qur'an, and learn Muslim history and culture, as well as studying typical school subjects.

Many Muslims feel that mixed-faith education causes problems for their children. For example, Islamic modesty means that many Muslim girls cannot wear shorts for sports and gym, or go swimming in mixed groups. Many schools do not serve halal food at lunch time. There are private Muslim schools and colleges, but only richer families can afford them.

A teacher asks questions during a class at a British Muslim school.

Problems students face

Life at school can be difficult for some Muslim pupils, especially if they have only recently arrived in Britain. They may not yet speak English well and have to learn about the British way of life, and find new friends. If they are refugees, they may still be suffering as a result of the terrible things they have seen in famine or war. In inner-city districts where many Muslim families live, some schools face problems, such as poor-quality buildings or a shortage of teachers. These problems can make learning even harder.

The school was built so Muslim children could learn about their own religion, culture and tradition in an environment that is supportive of those values. It is important for us to preserve our own distinct heritage and identity, and ensure there is adequate provision for personal, moral and social development within our own Islamic community.

Dr Musharaf Hussain,
Founder, Nottingham Islamia School.

Weddings and funerals

Traditionally, Muslims value marriage and family life a great deal. The Prophet Muhammad encouraged Muslims to marry, and taught children to love and respect their parents, especially their mothers. The Qur'an commands that Muslims show justice and kindness, and do good deeds for family members.

Marriage

In the past, Muslim marriages were arranged by parents for their children. Today, 49 per cent of young Muslim men in Britain and 67 per cent of young women are married to a partner chosen by their family. Before a wedding, the bride and groom usually meet and get to know each other, although older family members are often present, as well. Many Muslims happily take part in arranged marriages in which the couple and parents both agree on their choice of partner.

Some men marry women for their beauty, some for their wealth, but it is the best if you marry a woman who is a good Muslim.

Hadith (saying) of the Prophet Muhammad.

Muslim law allows men to have up to four wives, but UK law only allows marriage to one person at time.

Celebrations

Muslim families from different ethnic backgrounds celebrate weddings in different ways. Among British Muslims of Pakistani heritage, for example, celebrations can last for three days. They are held in town halls or community centres, and large numbers of family members, friends and other guests attend. The bride and groom – dressed in beautiful clothes – sit on a stage. They are asked three times in front of witnesses whether they wish to wed, and promise 'love, mercy, peace, faithfulness, cooperation and obedience to Allah'.

Mosques are holy places for worship and prayer, and many Muslims choose to get married in their local mosque.

Death

The Qur'an teaches that faithful Muslims will live after death in Paradise – and that sinners will be punished in Hell. When Muslims are near death, their carers encourage them to say the confession of faith, so they die speaking and thinking of Allah. After death, a Muslim's body is washed, wrapped in a cloth and then carried to a mosque for a funeral service. The imam leads prayers, asking for Allah's mercy and blessing on the dead person, and for help for all living Muslims to lead good lives. Then the body is buried in a graveyard. In Britain, some Muslims buy land and convert it into a Muslim graveyard. Muslims are also buried in Christian graveyards.

In many British cities, there are Muslim funeral directors who provide a traditional Islamic service for the Muslims in their community.

Focus on Nottingham

Nottingham, in the East Midlands, is an historic city, dating from medieval times. Today, Nottingham has a busy tourist industry and a lively multicultural community. In a national survey it was voted the best city in England to live in.

Arriving in Nottingham

Nottingham is home to around 267,000 people. About 12,400 (4.6 per cent) are Muslims. Most Muslim families came to Nottingham from Pakistan, after their homes were flooded by the Mangla Dam in the 1960s. Other families, from Pakistan's Rawalpindi region, worked for the British Army.

This Nottingham bookshop sells books in English, Arabic, and the other languages spoken by members of the local community.

At the Bobbersmill Community Centre plans to help local people are discussed.

Muslim community

To serve its Muslim community, Nottingham has eight mosques, the largest being the Islamic Centre. A community centre, in Bobbersmill, hosts a library, mosque, day nursery, Muslim radio station, sports facilities, women's groups, Qur'an lessons and classes where adults can learn Arabic, Islamic Studies and arts and crafts. Other community centres include the Pakistan Centre and the Kashmir Community College.

Youth

Nottingham has two Muslim schools, the Nottingham Islamia School and Jamia Al-Hudaa Girls' School. There are cricket and football teams, set up by the Bobbersmill Community Centre, that play in local leagues. In addition, organisations such as the Pakistan Centre and other small community groups work closely with Muslim youths.

Shops and organisations

Nottingham has halal butchers and takeaways, and shops selling food and clothes from abroad. Newsagents stock the *Daily Jang*, a Muslim newspaper written in Urdu and published in London. Nottingham is also home to 'Muslim Hands', an international charity that sends aid overseas, organises volunteer helpers and arranges welfare schemes.

We have worked hard to build up the Islamic School here in Nottingham. We aim to deliver a broad, balanced curriculum and to enable the pupils to develop to their highest capacity as servants of Allah.

Dr Musharraf Hussain, Founder, Nottingham Islamia School.

This store in Nottingham selling fresh fruit and vegetables is owned and run by a Muslim family.

Muslims at work

Some of the richest people in Britain are Muslims. There are around 5,400 British Muslim millionaires. For example, Sir Anwar Pervez came to Britain aged 21 and worked as a bus conductor. He now owns a cash and carry trading company worth over £220 million.

Unemployment

Muslims are also among Britain's poorest citizens. Many Muslim migrants to Britain, especially from Bangladesh and rural Pakistan, did not have the chance of higher education. The cities where they settled have also faced problems since they arrived, because of worldwide economic trends. Old factories have closed, along with many other businesses that supplied them. Muslim men in Britain are also much more likely to be unemployed – over 40 per cent of young Bangladeshi men cannot get a job, compared with 12 per cent of young, white British males.

This Muslim fast-food shop sells Asian foods such as samosas and curries as well as traditional British chips.

Self employment

Rich or poor, many Muslims work in the same sectors of the economy: fashion and textiles, buying and selling and food industries. There are over 6,000 Bangladeshi-owned restaurants in Britain, selling Asian-style food. Around 25 per cent of all Muslim men in Britain run their own small businesses, compared with only around 10 per cent of other British men.

Equal opportunities

In recent years, equal opportunities policies have created more job possibilities for Muslim workers. For example, Muslim men in the armed forces are no longer penalised for having beards, and female Muslim police officers are allowed to wear a hijab (headscarf).

Muslim bankers have also pioneered new ways of lending money without charging interest (forbidden by Islam) to help Muslims.

These two employees chat while they unroll some fabric for a customer to look at. This Muslim-owned shop sells hundreds of different styles and colours of fabric.

WORKING WOMEN

Only 2 out of every 10 British Muslim women work outside the home. Many Muslim women work 'behind the scenes' at family-run businesses and lots work very hard as full-time carers. But Muslim women's work is slowly changing. As more young Muslim women go to college and university, they look for work outside the home after they graduate.

Celebrating
and socialising

Muslim people in Britain often spend much of their free time with other members of the Muslim community. They meet through living in the same neighbourhood or by attending Muslim schools, community centres and mosques. They come together to share meals, especially at important Muslim religious festivals, or to celebrate the birth of a new baby.

Socialising

Most Muslim celebrations in Britain take place at home. Hospitality is a traditional duty (and pleasure). Since most Muslims do not drink alcohol, they usually do not go to pubs or bars. But in cities with large Muslim communities, such as Nottingham, London and Birmingham they can enjoy eating at Muslim-run vegetarian restaurants. Most Muslim community centres have rooms for large parties, and also run lunch clubs (for older people) and mother-and-toddler groups, where Muslim people can meet.

A Muslim girl proudly shows off the beautiful clothes she wears on special occasions.

THE MUSLIM CALENDAR

The Muslim calendar is based on observations of the Moon. It contains 354 days. This makes it 11 days shorter than the calendar used by the majority of Britons. Therefore, Muslim months – and Muslim festivals – fall at a different time each year.

Eid

For all Muslims, the two most important festivals are Eid ul-Fitr (at the end of the holy month of Ramadan) and Eid ul-Adha (Festival of Sacrifice), about 10 weeks later.

Eid ul-Fitr

Joyful Eid ul-Fitr celebrates the end of four weeks of fasting, and encourages feelings of peace, forgiveness and brotherhood. Children in Britain take the day off school. Friends and families meet to exchange good wishes and blessings. If they can, they put on new clothes and athar (perfume) and eat a special breakfast of thin noodles cooked in milk with nuts and raisins.

Eid ul-Adha

Eid ul-Adha is a solemn festival that commemorates the Prophet Ibrahim's willingness to sacrifice his son to Allah – and Allah's mercy in commanding him to kill a sheep, instead. Traditionally a whole sheep is sacrificed to share with the poor, family and friends. But today, many families in Britain celebrate Eid ul-Adha with prayers, parties and a special meal of lamb or mutton, and by giving money to charity.

Cards are sent to family and friends during Eid festivals. Eid Mubarak means 'Have a blessed holiday'.

Threats
and problems

Many British Muslims – especially Bangladeshi families, and refugees from Africa, the Middle East and the Balkans – live in inner-city districts. Eight out of every 10 Pakistani and Bangladeshi workers in Britain earn less than the national average wage.

In big cities, Muslims find few good jobs, overcrowded houses, over-stretched welfare and medical services, and, sometimes, problem schools. These difficulties would affect almost anyone who lived there, not just Muslims. But, because of poor homes and low income, people in the Muslim community have higher rates (20 per cent) of long-term illness than any other British community.

> **...racism is just another brand of unequal treatment. Inequality in our society is increasing, and for those at the bottom things are getting worse. Racism is our greatest challenge.**
>
> *Imran Khan, lawyer.*

Discrimination

Muslims are also more likely to suffer discrimination than Britons from any other religious or ethnic background. One in three Muslim people report that they or a member of their family have experienced personal abuse – either threatening words or gestures, or physical violence. Sometimes Muslims are abused for their faith; sometimes for their race or for their appearance.

Young Muslim men taking part – with Britons from many communities – in a march protesting against the war in Afghanistan, 2001.

Police stand guard as Muslim men pray in the street outside a London mosque, temporarily closed on 13 August, 2004. Many Muslims feel they are unfairly targeted due to their religious beliefs.

Terrorist attacks

Attacks on Muslims have become worse since terrorists attacked the USA on 11 September 2001, and British and US troops began their invasion of Afghanistan and Iraq. Peaceful, law-abiding Muslims find themselves treated with hatred and suspicion, as potential terrorists. Poor cities with Muslim communities have been targeted by extremist political parties. Some Muslim campaigners fear that new anti-terrorist rules made by the British government will limit Muslims' civil liberties.

Many Muslim people work hard to escape from poverty and combat racism. Some campaign to improve conditions; some protest angrily. In 2003, Muslim youths in Bolton (one of Britain's poorest cities) clashed with police after extremist political parties encouraged racial hatred between white and non-white communities during local election campaigns.

BARONESS UDDIN

Pola Uddin came to Britain from Bangladesh aged 13. In 1997 she became the first Muslim woman, and the first of Bangladeshi origin, to be made a baroness, and sit in the House of Lords. After training as a youth and community worker, Baroness Uddin campaigned for the rights of Bangladeshis, especially women in London's poor East End.

Future hopes and fears

Recent surveys of Muslim people in Britain reveal that, for many, their faith is the most important thing in their lives. They identify themselves as Muslims first, then as Britons.

These young girls hope for a bright future as members of the Muslim community in Britain.

Changing views

However, in the same surveys, Muslims said that they should do their best to integrate into British society – for example, by learning English and finding out about British laws. They are concerned that other people in Britain see them as 'different', or 'outsiders'. They hope these views will change.

Following the faith

There are also different views among Muslims about the best way to follow their faith in the modern world, and how to support their fellow-Muslims in war-torn overseas countries. Almost all Muslim leaders urge British Muslims to be moderate. They work with politicians and leaders of other faiths, hoping to bring peace and increase understanding. Most British Muslims support them.

Prince Charles meets young British Muslims at a party in his London palace, held to celebrate Eid ul-Fitr. Muslims are very much a part of British life.

Stereotyping

There are a few Muslims who hold different views from the majority of Muslims in Britain. They criticise social and political leaders in Europe and the USA. Often Muslims throughout Britain are wrongly associated with these few.

British society

The majority of British Muslims want to live peacefully alongside all other citizens of Britain. They value British traditions of tolerance and free speech, that allow them to practise their faith and work to play an important part in British society. They aim to be good Britons – and good Muslims, as well.

The Muslim and non-Muslim communities must look on each other as members of the same country, as human beings.

Zaki Badawi, Principal of the Muslim College in Britain.

Glossary

Arabic the holy language of Islam

Balkans the countries in the Balkan Peninsula, in south-eastern Europe

discrimination to treat people differently to others because of, for example, their race

Eid ul-Adha the festival of sacrifice which remembers the Prophet Ibrahim's willingness to sacrifice his son to Allah

Eid ul-Fitr a festival at the end of the holy month of Ramadan

ethnic belonging to a group through descent or culture

expel to drive somebody out by force

extremist somebody holding extreme political or religious beliefs

fast to go without anything to eat or drink for a certain period of time. Muslims also do good deeds as part of their fasting

free speech the right to express an opinion publicly

halal meat from animals that have been slaughtered in a way that abides by Islamic law

imam an Islamic religious leader

Indian subcontinent the region in Asia made up from the countries of Bangladesh, India, Pakistan and Sri Lanka

Islam the religion followed by Muslims and based on the teachings of the Prophet Muhammad

Makkah the Islamic holy city, in Saudi Arabia

Mangla Dam a dam built in Pakistan in the 1960s that created a reservoir that submerged around 250 villages in the Mirpur district and displaced 100,000 people

merchant somebody who buys and sells goods

Middle East the region stretching from the eastern Mediterranean to the western side of the Indian subcontinent

migrate to move from one place to another

mosque a Muslim place of worship

multicultural the mixing of cultures of different countries, ethnic groups or religions

Muslim somebody who follows the religion of Islam

persecution the cruel or unfair treatment of a group of people, often because of their ethnic origin or religious beliefs

Qur'an the Islamic holy book

Ramadan the month in the Islamic calender when Muslims fast during daylight hours. It was during this month that Muhammad first began to receive the message of Allah

refugee somebody who takes refuge from war or persecution by going to another country

ritual a procedure followed regularly and precisely, usually for religious purposes

sari a traditional garment worn by women in or from the Indian subcontinent, consisting of a length of fabric wrapped around the body

Further information

This is a selection of websites that may be useful for finding out further information on Islam and Muslims in Britain.

http://atschool.eduweb.co.uk/carolrb/islam/islamintro.html
general information on Islam

www.islamicgarden.com/page1002.html
a list of website links for Islamic children, or children wanting to know more about Islam

www.bbc.co.uk/religion/religions/islam/index.shtml
a BBC site on the religion and ethics of Islam

www.fairuk.org/dnd.htm
a site dealing with racism surrounding Islam

http://www.salaam.co.uk
an informative site about Muslims in Britain

http://www.redhotcurry.com
a lively news site about Asians in Britain, with information about music, films, sport, food, celebrities, etc

http://www.myh.org.uk/faithbased.htm
a Muslim Youth Helpsite, with information about issues facing Muslims in Britain

http://www.bbc.co.uk/gloucestershire/untold _stories/asian/gujurati_community.shtml
a BBC site telling the story of Muslims in Gloucestershire

Note to parents and teachers
Every effort has been made by the Publishers to ensure that these websites are suitable for children; that they are of the highest educational value, and that they contain no inappropriate or offensive material. However, because of the nature of the Internet, it is impossible to guarantee that the contents of these sites will not be altered. We strongly advise that Internet access is supervised by a responsible adult.

Index